## A New True Book

# THE BILL OF RIGHTS

### By Warren Colman

CHILDRENS PRESS ®

CHICAGO

The House of Representatives and the Senate meet in the Capitol.

PHOTO CREDITS

AP/Wide World Photos — 11 (left), 25 (right), 26 (2 photos), 28, 32 (bottom left and bottom right), 35, 40

᠌ Cameramann International, Ltd. — 19 (bottom right), 25 (left), 37 (right)

Marilyn Gartman Agency:
᠌ Herwig — 22 (right), 24 (right), 37 (left)
᠌ Michael P. Manheim — 17 (right)

Historical Pictures Service, Chicago — 10, 17 (left), 43

Journalism Services: ᠌ Paul F. Gero — 32 (top)

Nawrocki Stock Photo:
᠌ Robert Amft — 21 (left)
᠌ Rui Coutinho — 4 (top left)
᠌ Janet Davis — 19 (bottom left)
᠌ Robert Lightfoot — 23 (right)
᠌ Ken Love — 45
᠌ Ken Sexton — 23 (left), 24 (left)

North Wind Picture Archives — 13 (right), 29

Photo Source International: ᠌ Three Lions — 4 (top right), 9

H. Armstrong Roberts:
᠌ Camerique — 2, 38
᠌ Charles P. Cushing — 15
᠌ Scott Reed — 20 (middle)

Roloc Color Slides — 7, 11 (right), 13 (left), 16, 19 (top left), 20 (left), 22 (left)

Root Resources: ᠌ Mary Root — 19 (top right)

Tom Stack & Associates:
᠌ David M. Doody — Cover, 21 (right)
᠌ Tom Stack — 20 (right), 30

Art: M. Fiddle, 4 (bottom)

Cover: The Declaration of Independence, the Constitution, and the Bill of Rights on display in the National Archives, Washington, D.C.

Library of Congress Cataloging-in-Publication Data

Colman, Warren.
    The Bill of Rights.

    (A New true book)
    Includes index.
    Summary: A brief discussion of the meaning of the Bill of Rights, the first ten amendments of the Constitution of the United States.
    1.    United States — Constitutional law — Amendments — 1st-10th — Juvenile literature.    2.    Civil rights — United States — Juvenile literature.    [1.    United States — Constitutional law — Amendments — 1st-10th.    2.    Civil rights]    I.    Title.
KF4750.C574    1987        342.73′085        86-33437
ISBN 0-516-01232-0        347.30285

Childrens Press, Chicago
Copyright ᠌ 1987 by Regensteiner Publishing Enterprises, Inc.
All rights reserved. Published simultaneously in Canada.
Printed in the United States of America.
    3 4 5 6 7 8 9 10 R 96 95 94 93

# TABLE OF CONTENTS

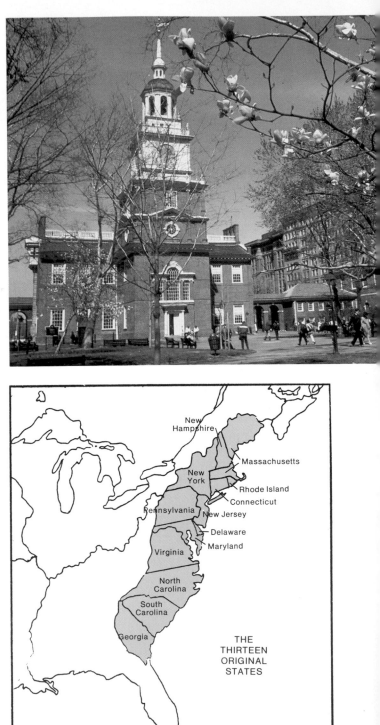

A copy of the Constitution (above). The constitutional convention met in Independence Hall (above right) in Philadelphia, Pennsylvania. Rhode Island was the only state that did not send delegates to the convention.

New Hampshire
Massachusetts
New York
Rhode Island
Connecticut
Pennsylvania
New Jersey
Delaware
Maryland
Virginia
North Carolina
South Carolina
Georgia

THE THIRTEEN ORIGINAL STATES

# TEN IMPORTANT PROMISES

In the United States, our most important law is the Constitution. It tells us how our government works. It lists our rights and liberties. All the laws in the United States must agree with the Constitution.

Two hundred years ago America was a very young country. There were thirteen states in the

United States. These states had agreed to work with each other.

In May 1787 leaders from twelve of the states met in Philadelphia. They worked all summer to write a plan for the new government. By September they were finished.

Thirty-nine men signed the Constitution. Then they brought it back to their states. Now the states had to vote for this new government.

Painting by H.C. Christy shows the delegates signing the Constitution. George Washington, standing at the desk, was president of the convention.

At first many states were not so sure that the Constitution was a good thing. They were afraid that it made the central government too powerful. Many Americans were afraid dishonest people might get in government.

Those people could then use their power to take away some of the freedoms that the American people felt belonged to them.

Many people said the Constitution did not say in words which rights belonged to the people and not to the government. People said these rights must be added to the Constitution. Only then would they vote for it.

James Madison understood why some states wanted changes made in the Constitution before they would accept it. He said, "In framing a system (the federal government) which we wish to last for all ages, we should not lose sight of the changes which ages will produce."

James Madison is called the "Father of the Constitution" because he worked so hard for it. Madison agreed that certain changes should be added to the Constitution.

When the Civil War ended in 1865, amendments had to be made to the Constitution. The Fourteenth Amendment gave the former slaves citizenship. The Fifteenth Amendment protected their right to vote. It said, no citizen should be denied the vote on account of race, color, or previous condition of servitude.

A list of ten rights was added to the Constitution in 1791. Because they protected the rights of all Americans they are called the Bill of Rights.

When something is added to the Constitution, it is called an amendment.

In 1918, 20,000 women marched in New York asking Congress to grant women the right to vote. The Nineteenth Amendment, passed in 1920, gave them this right.

I LOVE MY HUSBAND, BUT—
OH YOU VOTE

COPYRIGHTED          1909 BY DUNSTON-WEILER LITHOGRAPH C

In two hundred years our Constitution has had twenty-six amendments. All twenty-six are important. But many people believe the first ten—the Bill of Rights—are the most important.

# AN IMPORTANT IDEA

The Bill of Rights is based on the idea—that each person is important. So each person deserves certain rights.

Americans have always believed that each person is important. But for thousands of years, most people did not think this way.

In many places, they thought the only important person was the ruler—the king or queen. Almost

In 1776 supporters of the Declaration of Independence believed that Americans should no longer accept the rule of George III (left) and his parliament. In a public demonstration in New York City, colonists tore down the king's statue (right).

everyone else was seen as worthless. So the ruler could do whatever he or she wanted. A king or queen could take away someone's house. Or throw a person in jail. Or even kill someone.

But time after time people in other countries fought bad rulers. They fought for their rights. One of these fights happened in England.

In 1215, King John of England was forced to give certain rights to his dukes and barons. His written promise was called the *Magna Carta*. The *Magna Carta* was important. It showed that

The nobles in England forced King John to sign the Magna Carta.

other people, besides kings and queens, had certain rights.

Later, English laws gave other rights to the people. One law stated that English people did not

Colonists burned tax stamps. Throughout the colonies, people protested the right of the king and parliament in England to tax them.

have to pay unfair fines. By the 1600s, English laws promised many other freedoms to the people.

And so, when English and other European settlers came to America, they brought along some

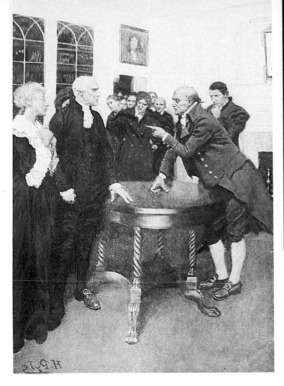

Colonists (left) asked representatives of King George for their right to take part in the government of the colonies. These peaceful discussions failed. Even today, Americans remember the more violent acts of rebellion, such as the Boston Tea Party.

strong beliefs. One was that all people, being worthwhile, deserve certain rights.

Many of those rights are found in the first ten amendments of our Constitution.

# FOUR IMPORTANT FREEDOMS

The First Amendment gives us four important freedoms.

- We may worship as we please.
- We may gather to discuss peaceful ways to change unfair laws.
- We are entitled to a free press.
- We may speak openly about what we think and feel.

## *Freedom of Religion*

At one time, most countries in Europe had one main religion. It was called the "official church." People who didn't worship at that church sometimes couldn't have certain jobs. Sometimes they were jailed.

The authors of the Bill of Rights thought that nobody should be punished for his or her religious beliefs.

Top left: Russian Orthodox Church in Washington, D.C.
Top right: Baha'i Temple, Wilmette, Illinois
Bottom left: Congregational Church, Oak Park, Illinois
Bottom right: Islamic Center in Washington, D.C.

Above: Synagogue in Washington, D.C.
Right: First Baptist Church in Tennessee
Far right: Roman Catholic Church in New Mexico

And so the First Amendment says the United States cannot have an official religion. It also says Americans may worship as they please.

*Freedom of Assembly*

Americans have always believed that it is often

wise to meet to discuss ways of making things better.

Our forefathers knew that no government is perfect. Sometimes laws don't work well. They need to be fixed. They

Peace march (left) and people protesting the political beliefs of the Nazi Party and the Ku Klux Klan (below). Americans have always demonstrated in support of their political causes.

Anti-nuke demonstrators (above) and supporters of the War on Poverty (left).

understood that people had to meet to discuss these changes.

The First Amendment says Americans may gather "peaceably." It also says that Americans can tell their government what changes they want made.

The First Amendment gives all
Americans freedom of speech.

## *Freedom of Speech*

Besides talking about
changing laws, Americans
are free to talk about
other matters. The First
Amendment states that we
have freedom of speech.
We are allowed to voice

our opinion on almost
anything we wish.

Even so, our freedom of
speech is limited. For
example, we may not shout
"fire" in a theater when
there is no fire. People
could panic and someone
might be trampled.

## Freedom of the Press

Americans may *write* about whatever they wish, too—in books, newspapers, and magazines. Reporters may write whatever they want. We call this "freedom of the press."

In some countries,

Newspapers have the freedom to print what they want without seeking the approval of the government.

The official newspaper in Russia is *Pravda*. In many countries the newspapers may only report the news that the government wants reported.

reporters are not allowed to write what they want. The government stops them. In those countries, it is hard for people to discover the truth. They cannot find out all the facts. They learn only the facts the government wants them to know.

# SAFE HOMES, SAFE COUNTRY

The Second, Third, and Fourth Amendments assure that Americans live in safety.

*Right to Bear Arms*

The Second Amendment says people may keep guns.

Today many people believe guns and rifles are dangerous. They say not everyone should be

Demonstrators picket in support of laws that would deny individuals the right to own handguns.

allowed to have them in their homes.

But other people say Americans have the right to keep guns. They say a person has the right to protect himself or herself with a gun.

Before the Revolutionary War, the British government sent soldiers to keep order in the colonies. The citizens of Boston were forced to house and feed these soldiers in their homes.

## *No Soldiers in Homes*

When England ruled America, British soldiers were sometimes placed in the colonists' homes. Most Americans disliked having the soldiers in their houses.

United States soldiers

The Third Amendment
says soldiers may not be
placed in our homes
during times of peace. But
it says that could change
if there is a war.

## No Unreasonable Searches

In some countries, the police can enter and search a person's home at any time. And they can take away a person's belongings any time they want.

In those countries, soldiers can stop any person on the street. They can search that person any time they want.

Those soldiers and police officers do not need

Police dog (above) demonstrates its ability to sniff out explosives. The rights in the Bill of Rights were written to protect citizens from being sent to concentration camps as were the political prisoners (right) under Hitler's Nazi rule in Germany. Unfortunately, these rights have been violated in recent years. During World War II American citizens of Japanese descent (below) were sent to camps without fair trials.

a reason to make searches.
They can just do it.

But not in the United
States.

The Fourth Amendment
prevents officials from
unfairly searching homes
and persons. If police
officers search your house,
they must first get
permission from a judge.
The police must convince
the judge they have a
good reason to enter your
home.

# PROTECTING ACCUSED PERSONS

The authors of the Bill of Rights gave much thought to the subject of fair trials.

In fact, almost half of the Bill of Rights discusses the rights of people accused of a crime.

In some countries, governments can get rid of their enemies by

Winnie Mandela is the wife of Nelson Mandela who has been in a South African prison for decades because of his political opinions. Many people see this as an example of a government's misuse of political power.

sending them to jail. The government just says, "That person has committed a crime."

The person may be innocent. But it doesn't matter. Without fair trials, it's easy to put an innocent person in jail.

## *Fifth Amendment Rights*

The Fifth Amendment promises certain rights to accused persons.

- When a person is accused of a serious crime, his case usually must go to a *grand jury* first. This group decides if there's enough evidence for a trial to begin.
- A person normally can't go to trial more than once for the same crime.
- A person can't be forced to testify against himself or herself.
- All laws must be followed during a trial.

## *Sixth Amendment Rights*

The Sixth Amendment grants six rights to

# accused persons. All people accused of a crime

- are entitled to a speedy trial. The trial cannot be held in secret.
- can choose to have their case decided by a jury.
- must be told what crime they have supposedly committed.
- must be able to see and hear the people who have accused them.
- have the right to have witnesses who can prove their innocence.
- may have a lawyer.

In America all people accused of a crime have a right to just and speedy trial.

A judge addresses the court.

## *Seventh Amendment Rights*

Not all trials are for crimes. Sometimes people go to court to settle arguments. The Seventh Amendment says all laws must be followed in non-criminal trials. It also says that an accused person in most non-criminal trials can ask for a jury trial.

*Eighth Amendment Rights*

In America, a person is innocent until proven guilty. So it wouldn't be fair to keep an accused person in jail until his trial is over. Most people accused of a crime are allowed to go home.

A lawyer asks the judge to set bail for his client.

But to make certain they do not run away, accused persons must give the court bail money. They get this money back when they return to trial.

The Eighth Amendment says that the bail cannot be too high. This right protects innocent people

from staying in jail until
they have had their trial.

If a person must pay a
fine, it cannot be too high,
either. The Eighth Amendment
forbids unfair fines.

Finally, the Eighth
Amendment forbids cruel
or unusual punishments. In
some countries, if a
person is caught stealing,
one of his hands may be
cut off. In America, that
would be a cruel
punishment. It is forbidden
by the Bill of Rights.

# REMAINING RIGHTS

The authors of the Bill
of Rights knew they
couldn't list every right. So
the Ninth Amendment says
that all rights not listed
in the Constitution or the
Bill of Rights belong to
the people. It also says
that the government
cannot deny those rights
to any person.

The Tenth Amendment
was written to keep the
government from becoming

The Bill of Rights includes the first ten amendments to the Constitution of the United States.

too powerful. It says the federal government may have *only* the powers given to it by the Constitution. All other powers are given to the states and the people.

# THE BILL OF RIGHTS PROTECTS US

We have had the Bill of Rights for a long time. So it's easy to take it for granted.

But just imagine how terrible life might be if we could not worship as we please. Or if we were not able to write and speak freely.

Think how awful it would be if we were not

In order to protect our rights every
citizen must vote and take part in government.

protected from being
thrown in jail unfairly!
    The Bill of Rights stops
those things from happening.
    The Bill of Rights protects
all of us!

# WORDS YOU SHOULD KNOW

**accuse**(ah • KYOOZ) — inform one of an error, a crime, or other wrongdoing

**amendment**(ah • MEND • mint) — a statement with changes, corrections or improvements upon the original

**assure**(ah • SHOOR) — to make sure, without doubt

**baron**(BAIR • un) — In Great Britain, the lowest ranking noble who holds land granted by the king

**beliefs**(bih • LEEFS) — something that is believed to be truth, without having positive proof or knowledge of

**bill**(BIHL) — an official written document describing a law or some important formal statement

**central**(SEN • tril) — main, chief; the important part

**committed**(kah • MIT • id) — done, performed

**duke**(DOOK) — In Great Britain nobility, a male member in the royal family line, just under a prince

**effort**(EF • ert) — work; time or energy spent for some reason

**federal**(FED • er • il) — the central part of the government made up of the combined states

**framing**(FRAY • ming) — putting into words; designing a plan, creating

**grants**(GRANTS) — awards, gives

**jury**(JOO • ree) — a group of people appointed in a court to hear the trial of a case and to decide on the guilt or innocence of the accused

**liberty**(LIB • er • tee) — freedom; being able to act, speak, worship, work according to one's choice

**nobility**(no • BIL • ih • tee) — line of highest regarded persons; first, those descended from royal families; second, their descendants; third, persons not related but next in regard depending on high quality of birth, position, rank, or title

**official**(oh • FISH • il) — authorized

**panic**(PAN • ik) — to be overcome by a sudden and intense fear

**rights**(RITES) — that to which anyone is entitled; just, morally and legally correct

**system**(SIS • tim) — a method of instructions, plans, ideas, that forms an orderly pattern to work from

# INDEX

*About the author*

*Warren Colman is a writer-director-producer. He is president of a company that makes educational filmstrips and videos, as well as training and promotional media for businesses. He has a bachelor's and a master's degree from Northwestern University.*